A DOZEN A DAY
VIOLIN

To access audio visit:
www.halleonard.com/mylibrary

5859-9532-8961-2333

All exercises and engravings created by Camden Music.
Backing tracks composed and arranged by Jeremy Birchall and Christopher Hussey.
Violin by Alexandra Wood.
Recordings produced, mixed and mastered by Jonas Persson.
Design and illustrations by Ruth Keating.
Printed in the EU.

ISBN 978-1-78038-368-2

EXCLUSIVELY DISTRIBUTED BY

HAL•LEONARD®

Visit Hal Leonard Online at
www.halleonard.com

World headquarters, contact:
Hal Leonard
7777 West Bluemound Road
Milwaukee, WI 53213
Email: info@halleonard.com

In Europe, contact:
Hal Leonard Europe Limited
1 Red Place
London, W1K 6PL
Email: info@halleonardeurope.com

In Australia, contact:
Hal Leonard Australia Pty. Ltd.
4 Lentara Court
Cheltenham, Victoria, 3192 Australia
Email: info@halleonard.com.au

A DOZEN A DAY
VIOLIN

Pre-Practice
Technical Exercises
FOR THE VIOLIN

THE WILLIS MUSIC COMPANY

A DOZEN A DAY
VIOLIN

Having a secure technique is vital for becoming a good musician, but with regular practice comes the need for regular warm-ups. Edna-Mae Burnam's much-loved *A Dozen A Day* series has been adapted for the violin, with new exercises and fun backing tracks to ensure students maintain their daily warm-ups.

These exercises are designed to promote good habits in bowing and fingering, as well as interval recognition ('steps', 'hops'). Students are strongly recommended to sing these exercises whilst fingering on the fingerboard before attempting them with the bow, in order to gain a mental picture of how the notes should sound—this will encourage focused pitching and musical phrasing.

Do not try to learn the entire first dozen exercises the first week you study this book! Just learn two or three exercises, and do them each day *before* practising. When these are mastered, add another, then another, and keep adding until the twelve can be played perfectly.

Remember that a daily routine of technical exercises will give you the tools to make beautiful music.

Contents

Group I

Group II

Group III

Group IV

Group V

Group I

1. Walking, Jogging And Running

2. Jogging Up A Hill

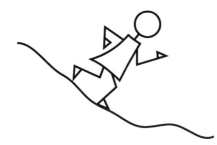

3. Running Down A Hill

4. Stretching Right Leg

5. Stretching Left Leg

6. Jumping (Left-Hand Pizzicato)

7. Press-Ups

8. Up On Tiptoes

9. Rolling

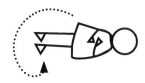

10. Jumping

11. Stretching Up

12. Fit As A Fiddle

Fit as a fid-dle, I keep my fin-gers strong. Fit as a fid-dle, sing and play a song.

Group II

1. Walking And Jogging

2. Hopping

3. Deep Knee Bend

4. Running On Tiptoe

5. Rocking

6. Swaying

7. Cartwheels

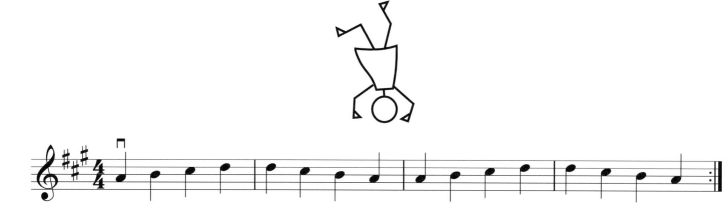

8. High Stepping

9. Forward Rolls

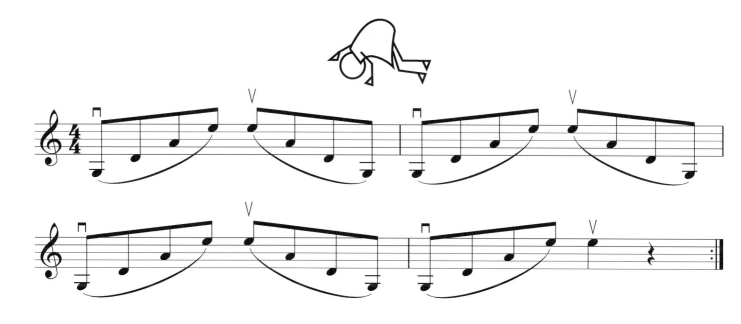

10. Jumping

11. Climbing A Ladder

12. Fit As A Fiddle

Fit as a fid - dle, all day long. Ex - er - cise will make my fin - gers strong.

Group III

1. Walking Up A Hill, Running Down

2. Rocking

3. Bouncing A Ball

4. Throwing A Ball

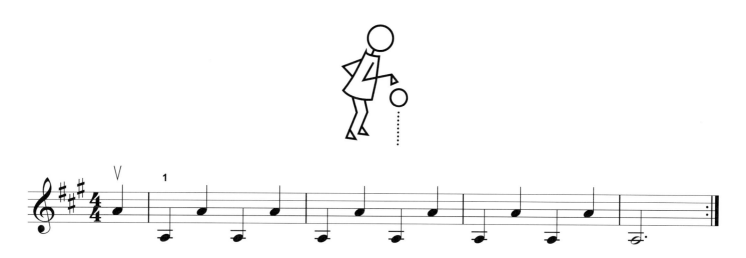

5. Rolling A Ball

6. Deep Knee Bend

7. Giant Steps

8. Jogging

9. Swaying

10. Climbing A Ladder

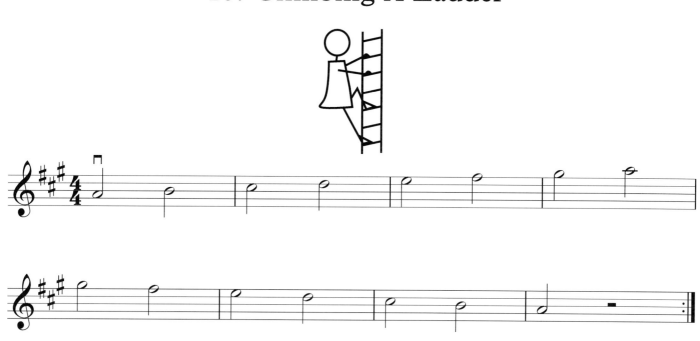

11. Swinging Arms

12. Fit As A Fiddle

Fit as a fid - dle, ex - er - cise my fin - gers ev - 'ry day.

Fit as a fid - dle, ex - er - cise will make my fin - gers play.

Group IV

1. Deep Breaths

2. Up On Tiptoes

3. Stretch And Bend

4. A Clever Trick

5. Leg Work (Lying Down)

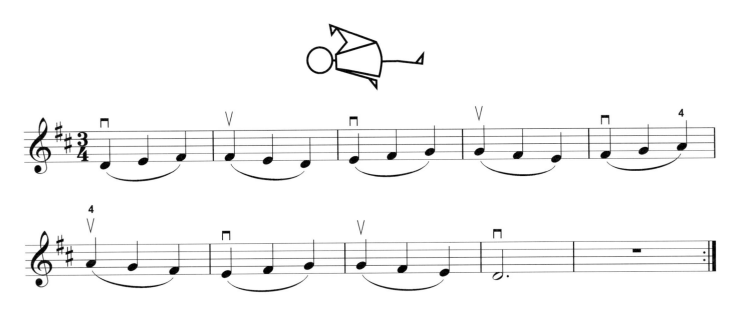

6. Twisting The Swing, Then It Unwinds

7. Swinging Arms

8. Handsprings

9. Rolling

10. Hopscotch

11. Cartwheels

12. Fit As A Fiddle

If I do my doz-en a day, from top to toe and the mid - dle,

then I'll know I'll al - ways stay just as fit as a fid-dle!

Group V

1. Up And Down The Slide

2. Baby Steps

3. On Tiptoes

4. Touching Toes

5. Deep Breaths

6. Hopping

7. Jogging Up A Hill On A Sunny Day, Then A Cloudy Day

8. Walking On A Sunny Day, Then A Cloudy Day

9. Climbing Further Up The Hill

10. Marching

11. A Clever Trick

12. Fit As A Fiddle

A doz - en a day be - fore I play

keeps mis - takes a - way. A doz - en a day, hip

hip hoo - ray, makes me feel O - K!

Track Listing

Each track is split—hear both violin and accompaniment if the balance is centred,
and the accompaniment only if the balance control is to the right!